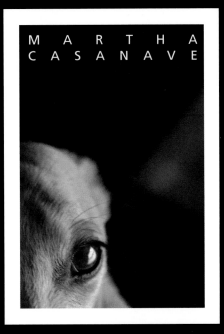

MARTHA
CASANAVE

# BEWARE OF DOG
## YOU MIGHT FALL IN LOVE

# MARTHA CASANAVE

# BEWARE OF DOG

## YOU MIGHT FALL IN LOVE

Introduction by
HUNTINGTON WITHERILL

CENTER FOR PHOTOGRAPHIC ART
CARMEL, CALIFORNIA

# INTRODUCTION
by HUNTINGTON WITHERILL

*If you pick up a starving dog and make him prosperous, he will not bite you.*
*This is the principle difference between a dog and a man.*

– Mark Twain

*I have sometimes thought of the final course of dogs having such short lives*
*and I am quite satisfied it is in compassion to the human race; for if we suffer*
*so much in loving a dog after an acquaintance of ten or twelve years,*
*what would it be if they were to live double that time?*

– Sir Walter Scott

One summer evening a few years back, while seated among several dinner guests at Martha Casanave's home, our hostess suggested that for the remainder of the evening we assume a new identity. We were invited to adopt a new first name based upon the name of a family pet when we were children. And our last name would become the name of the street on which we had lived. As we went around the table I quickly realized I was soon to be known as "Rebel Latimer."

Rebel was a handsome German Shepherd of unusually noble descent. When he arrived at out doorstep in 1960, my older brother had announced with the kind of authority only an older brother can muster that Rebel was one of the true great-grandsons of the original film star, Rin Tin Tin. Of course, the relative accuracy of this pronouncement was of no concern to me. We had a celebrity in our midst!

"Rinty," as he was affectionately known to film audiences, had made his acting debut in the 1922 silent feature: *The Man From Hell's River.* Born on September 12, 1918, in France, his story had been one of rags-to-riches. Having been rescued from a bunker by an American airman at the conclusion of World War I, this four-legged performer's eventual box-office clout earned him the studio nickname: "the mortgage lifter." Rinty had saved many a neighborhood movie house from closure during the Great Depression. When he died on August 8, 1932 in Beverly Hills, California, it was reported that he had his own production unit, a private limousine with chauffeur, a personal chef to prepare chateaubriand at mealtimes, and his own orchestra for mood music! Ahhh... the trappings of stardom. My introduction to Rinty's great-grandson was to be one of my first brushes with fame.

Owing to his obvious aristocratic ancestry, Rebel instantly and effortlessly demonstrated his enormous capacity for true companionship and unquestioning devotion. It was a bond for life. Sadly, though, it was a bond for Rebel's life. I would too quickly learn that the loss of my cherished friend was to be a thoroughly crushing blow from which, as any dog lover knows, I could only survive by the adoption of another dog.

Three dogs have lovingly shared their lives with me over the past forty years. Thus, it is with shameless self-professed authority, based upon solid experience, that I can proclaim my qualifications to declare Martha Casanave in possession of an unusually clear and deep-rooted understanding regarding the essence of that powerfully emotional bond between a dog and its master.

Casanave's photographs in BEWARE OF DOG exhibit a remarkable directness and immediacy. The experience of her background as a portrait photographer brings with it an uncanny ability to instinctively target the very heart and soul of her subject matter. Attempting to visually communicate a labyrinth of circumstances comprising that magical bond between human and animal is no small feat. Yet, like many great artists, Casanave seems able to accomplish her artistic challenge with ease. BEWARE OF DOG is its own rags-to-riches story, complete with humbly unsettled beginnings, a persistence of determination, and the inevitable auspicious ending which leaves the viewer filled with feelings of reassurance and hope for the future.

As a photographer, Martha Casanave has consistently used her outstanding perceptual intuition to effectively communicate a genuine passion for her subjects, and BEWARE OF DOG is no exception. Though the individual portraits in this book each display a distinctive style and substance, it is the overall sequence of images which serves to clarify and communicate a most compelling story about the life and times of both the photographer and her canine companion. The symbiotic relationship in which Casanave and her dog assist one another in overcoming life's adversity, and the triumph of spirit and transformation that both experience through the process, makes for a truly moving photographic essay.

I've always been a sucker for anything with four legs and fur. BEWARE OF DOG tugs at my heart-strings just like Rebel and Rin Tin Tin did when I was a kid. Through the magic of her extraordinary photographic transformations, Casanave has unveiled a story which not only celebrates the exquisitely sublime nature of the companionship between one woman and her dog, but also serves as a befitting tribute to the singular friend who led her toward salvation.

– Rebel Latimer

# BEWARE OF DOG

by MARTHA CASANAVE

When I told my mother I was going to get a dog, she said she'd never have a dog again. "I wouldn't want to lose it," she said, remembering our family dog from years ago. "I loved that old dog," she said, her eyes brimming. It was that brief conversation I recalled when I decided to call this series of photographs BEWARE OF DOG.

*   *   *

I adopted a whippet in 1992, a time when I was fatigued with an undiagnosed illness. I spoke to few people about my illness, because it didn't have a name. Outside of work, I kept myself isolated as much as possible so people wouldn't notice how I was feeling. I wanted an animal for companionship.

My two-year old whippet came to me sight unseen, by air, in a crate. I had made arrangements to adopt her by long distance telephone. Unbeknownst to me, she also was ill. She was lethargic and underweight. She had been moved around frequently, and was anxious and depressed. She was agoraphobic: seeing her leash made her tremble with dread. Like me, she didn't like being out in the world. She exhibited signs of earlier abuse and had a huge scar from a ligament injury. She didn't play, or even wag her tail. She was afraid of men. She was terrified of all other dogs. So here we were: a couple of basket cases.

Over time, we got used to each other. She gradually became healthy, and more gradually became happy and secure. In 1996, my illness was finally diagnosed, and I began treatment. That day, the day I came home from the hospital, with electrode "X's" still marked on my body, was the day I began photographing my dog. I wasn't thinking of a series. I just wanted to use my camera to celebrate my dog for her companionship during those dark years. But that one picture started a flow of images about our life together.

Later, as medication brought my life back to normal, I began photographing the whippet playing ball with me outdoors, as if her speed and exuberance symbolized my own returning energy.

*   *   *

There are many things a black and white photograph cannot communicate. The true grandeur of a landscape, for example. It cannot convey the endless expanse, the feeling of wind, the scent of sage, the rough feel of a rock warmed by the sun, the smell of rain in the air, or the sound of distant thunder.

Likewise, a photograph cannot tell a viewer about the velvety feel of a whippet's belly skin. Or the heat emanating from its 102-degree body. Or the delicate smell of its soft fur. The pungent odor of dog footpads. The sound of shaking ears (like little furiously flapping rags), of a tongue lapping water, or of feet galloping down a carpeted hallway. Or the feel on one's arm of the small hot breath of a sleeping whippet. In the dark of night a dreaming dog makes the bed shake like an earthquake does – what can a photograph say about that?

*   *   *

Doing the photographs has been as important to me – perhaps more important – than looking at them. The process of paying close attention to every detail of my dog and watching her behavior closely has caused me to find more joy in quotidian things, to be more conscious of being fully present. How many people do you know who leap with joy and shout "Yippee!" after going to the bathroom? It is, a dog can teach you, a wonderful thing when your bowels move as they are supposed to. And how many times would I have marvelled at the way light filters through an ear, or the way fur grows in lovely swirling patterns, if I hadn't been studying these things with my camera?

Doing a series like this teaches that one doesn't have to go anywhere to find photographs. It sharpens one's visual sense wherever one happens to be.

*   *   *

Indolence and exuberance: the life-pattern of a whippet. Whippets, like cats, enjoy long periods of sloth-like indolence. They find the most comfortable place in the house to sleep. No amount of training can keep a whippet off soft things. If the soft thing is in a patch of warm sunshine or near a crackling fireplace, so much the better. Whippets are heat-seeking units. The periods of sloth are regularly punctuated with short bursts of hysterical, exuberant activity. You know when one of those bursts is coming: you can see the crazed look and the flaring nostrils. My whippet does high-speed circles in the house or yard, with her hind end going faster then her front end. Or else she brings me a tennis ball and performs high vertical leaps until I consent to play with her. After the bout of play, she flops down somewhere comfortable again, heaves a big breath, and flutters her eyelids closed.

*   *   *

Having a dog and paying close attention to her with my camera has also made me acutely aware of the awesome nature of power over a dependent creature. Discipline, consistency and respect must accompany that power. I see all around me, with both children and animals, how power over an inferior can make people forget their responsibility. The neglectful, accidental death by hanging of a Rottweiler who lived behind our house is an extreme, horrifying example. But such examples abound in our world.

*   *   *

"My dog." "My husband." "My wife." "My child." Until you have these things, and develop a bond, saying the words feels strange. I practiced saying "my dog" – and laughed self-consciously – for weeks before she arrived.

*   *   *

The nature of the bonding that happens with a dog, as between people, has much to do with familiarity. It can't be rushed or forced. The longer you live together, the more you intuitively understand each other. You anticipate the other's needs, wants and moods, and unwittingly develop a kind of synchrony. Bonding depends on all the senses. Sometimes when I am away from my whippet, I think I catch a whiff of her. Phantom-scent. It tugs my heart home. You can't resist this kind of bonding, it happens like it or not. And it's this kind of bonding which makes separation or loss so painful. It's what my mother was talking about.

*   *   *

Sometimes I feel twinges of guilt when I am travelling because I seem to miss my dog more than I miss my person. But when I think about this peculiar phenomenon of feeling, I realize that there is a sound reason for it. I speak with my partner by telephone every day. He knows I am thinking about him, and I know he is thinking about me. He knows when I am coming home. My dog, though well cared for when I am away, doesn't know when I am coming home. My scent is everywhere in the house, but how is she to know if I am coming home at all? When I think about that, I can feel her sense of loss, and I miss her very much. When I do come home she is deliriously happy for a short while, and then becomes (what seems to me) depressed and a little confused for a day. I imagine that she is thinking: "How long will you stay? When will you leave again? Should I be vigilant and reserved?" Travelling is much harder for me, now that I have a dog.

\* \* \*

When I've been out for an evening, my dog always smells what's different about me. She checks my breath first. I assist her by breathing into her face and saying "Yep! Garlic breath!" Or, "Yep! Garam masala breath!" Then she checks my clothing and shoes. Some of the first photographs I made of my dog were of her needle nose.

\* \* \*

Doing these photographs has made me more aware of the fleeting nature of time. My whippet was younger than I was when we began these pictures. I like to believe we are growing old together. But she is much older than I am now...

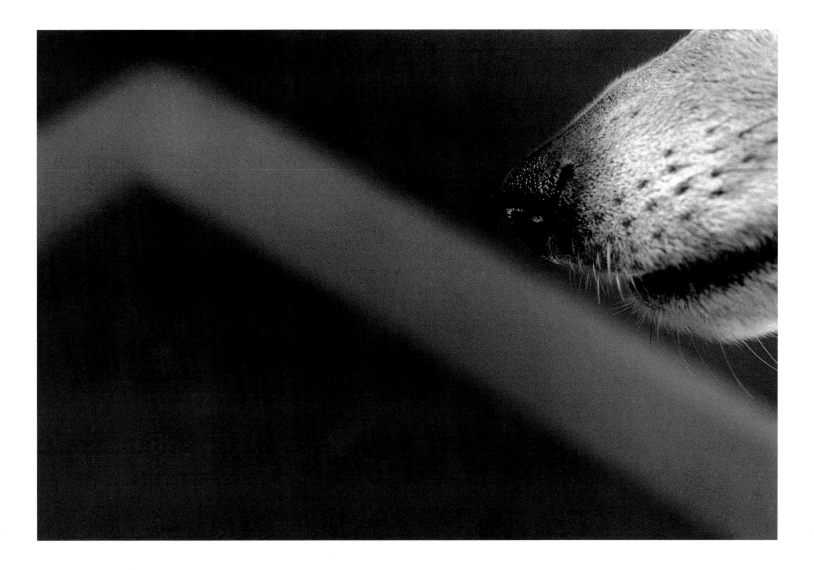

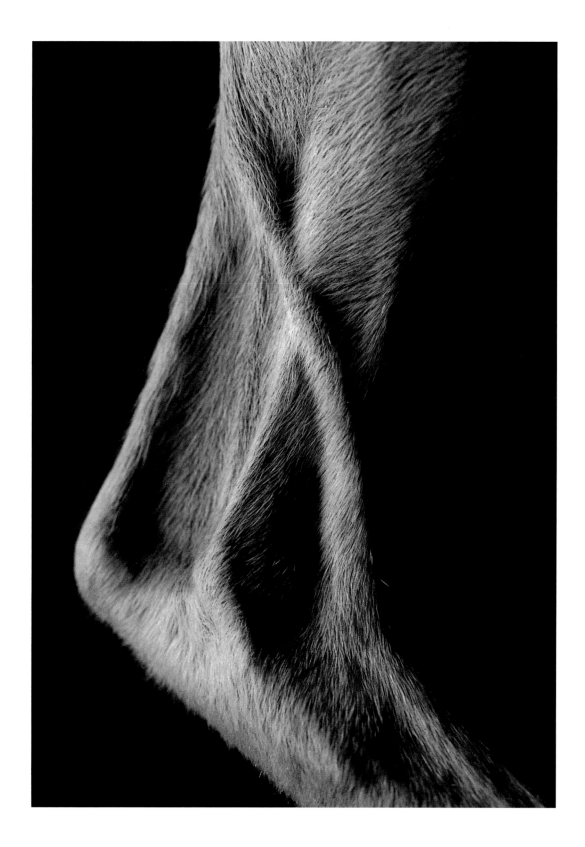

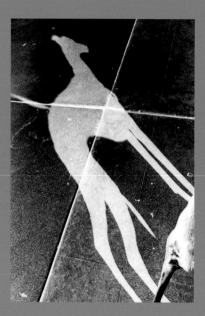

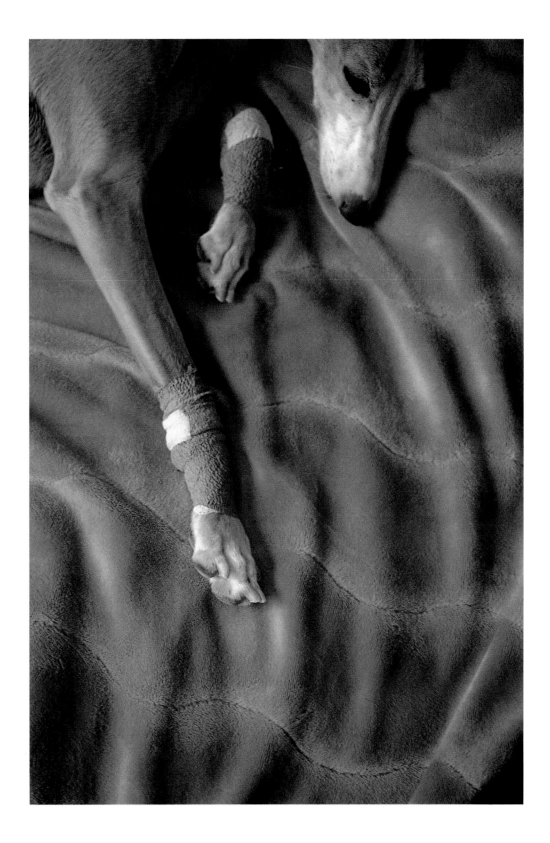

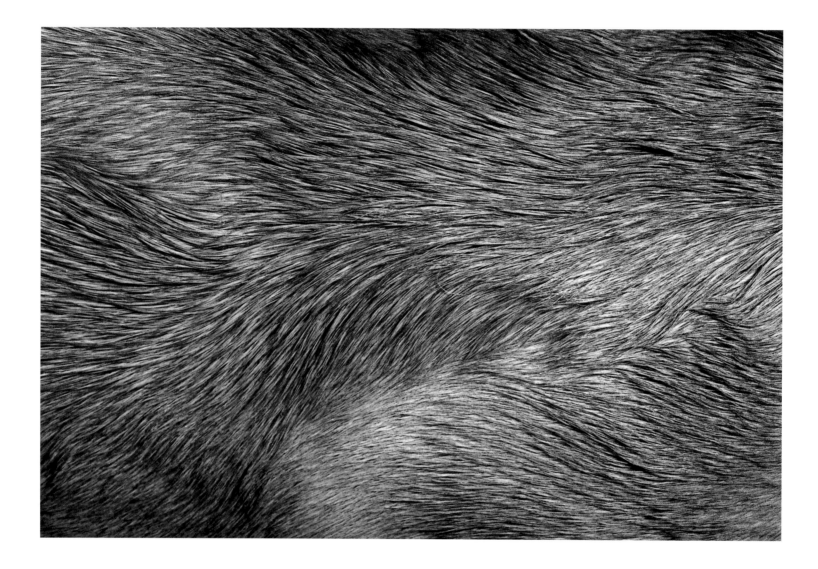

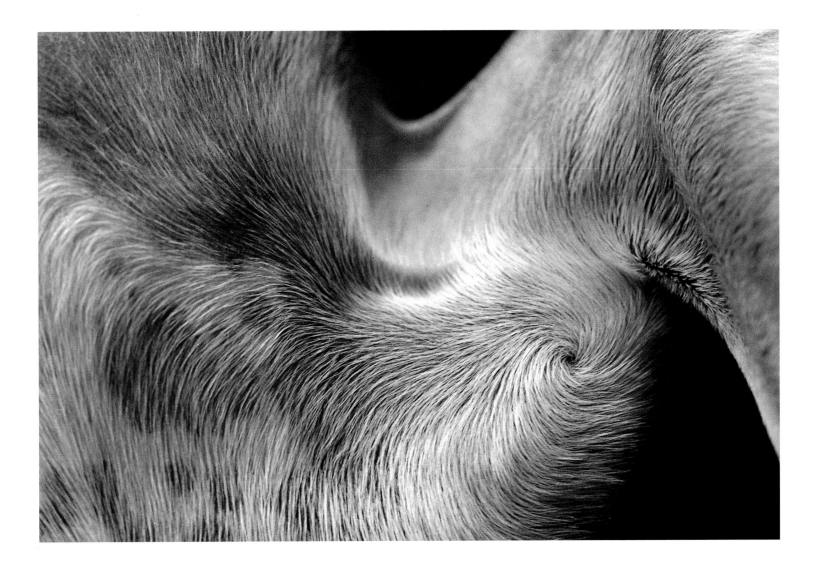

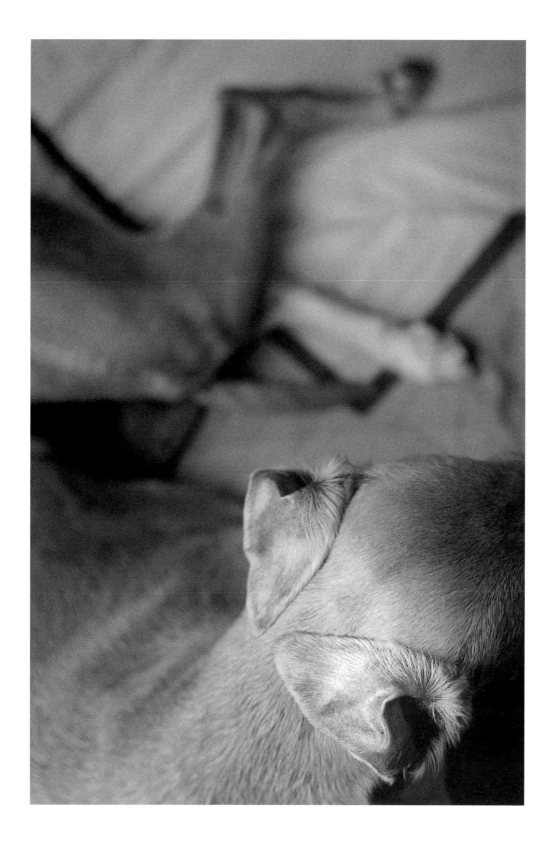

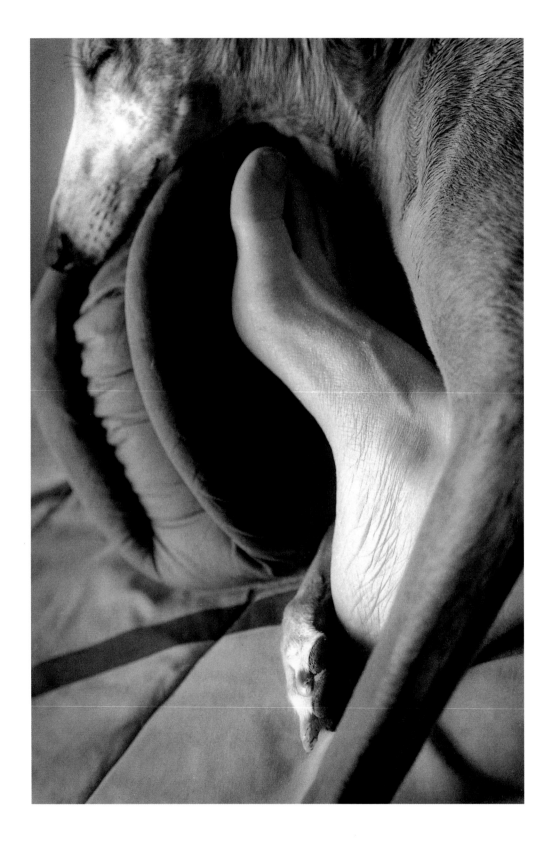

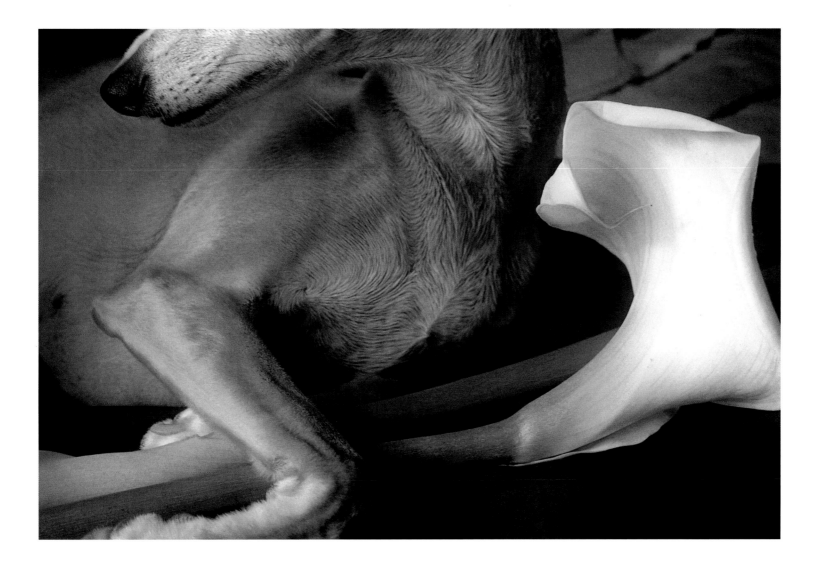

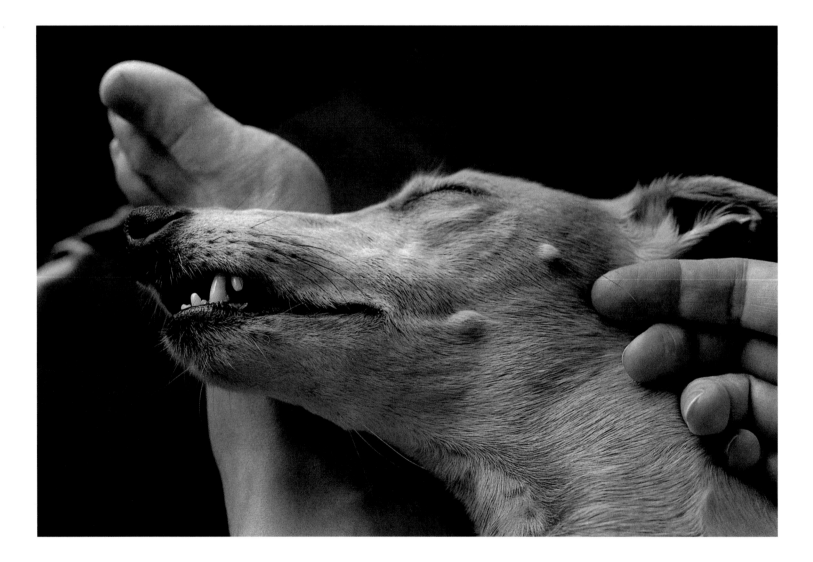

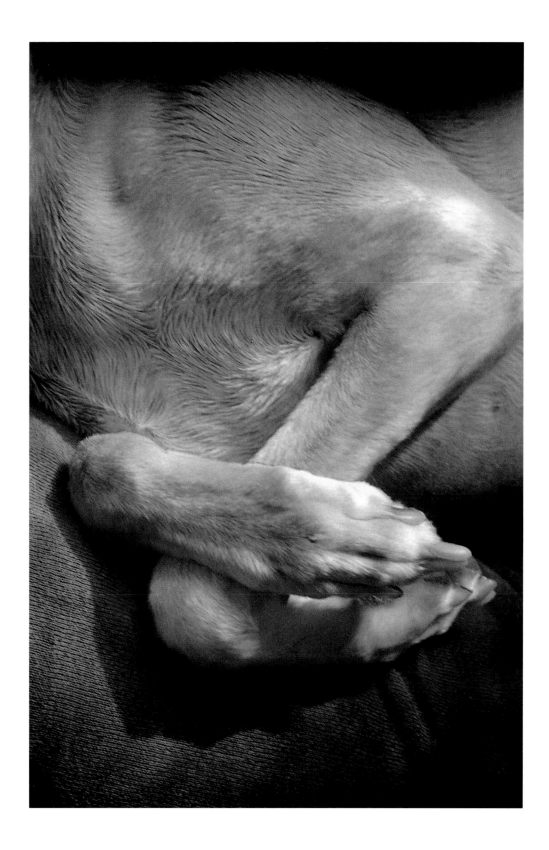

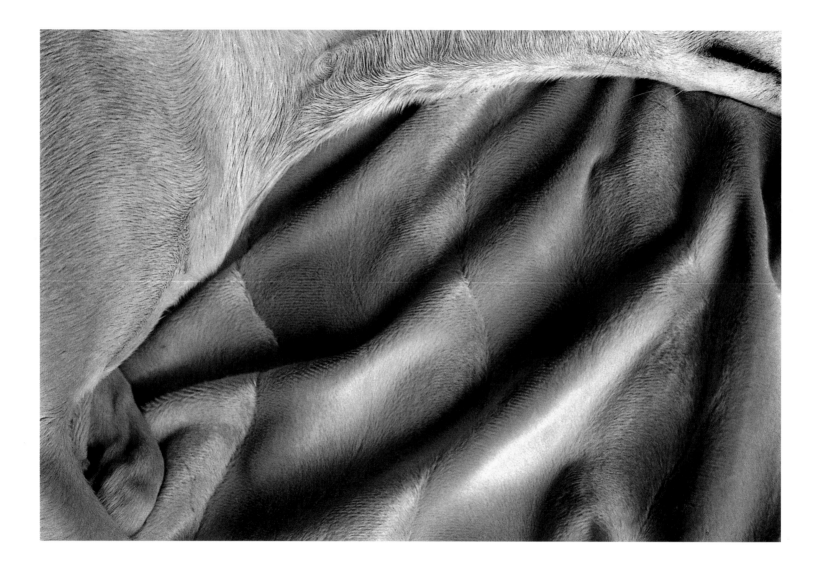

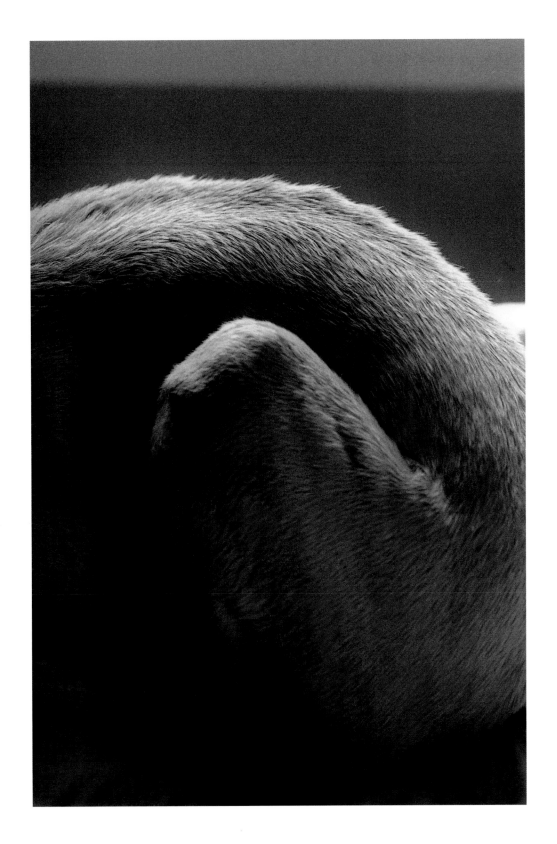

# ACKNOWLEDGEMENTS

With immense gratitude, I would like to acknowledge the generous support of the many friends and relatives who supported this project; special thanks go to the following, without whom this book would not have been possible:

| | |
|---|---|
| *Christine Casanave* | *Jane Olin* |
| *N. Brooke Gabrielson* | *Gordon F. Pearson* |
| *Chip Hooper* | *Dr. Dilip Raval* |
| *Stu Levy and Cris Maranze* | *Anna Rheim* |
| *Jack Klein* | *Studio BP, Inc.* |
| *Jane K. Lombard* | *John Schatz* |
| *David McCrae and* | *Neil Shapiro* |
| *Suzanne Schweitzer* | *Bob Wecker* |
| *Marcia Millen* | *Anonymous* |

I would also like to thank *Dennis High,* Executive Director of the Center for Photographic Art in Carmel, for his enthusiastic support and for his careful and attentive coordination of this project; *Bert Ihlenfeld* for his superb design; *Charlie Clarke* of C&C Offset for his guidance through the printing process; my partner *Ryuijie* for his enduring patience and support; and of course I thank my pal *Sweet Pea,* who opened my heart and teaches me daily what it means to be alive, responsive, and responsible.

FIRST EDITION 2002

Photographs © Copyright 2002 Martha Casanave
Introduction © Copyright 2002 Huntington Witherill

ISBN 0-9630393-8-5
Library of Congress Catalog Card Number 2002004678

   Library of Congress Cataloging-in-Publication Data
Casanave, Martha.
   Beware of dog : you might fall in love / by Martha Casanave ; introduction by Huntington Witherill.-- 1st ed.
      p. cm.
   ISBN 0-9630393-8-5
 1. Whippet--Anecdotes. 2. Whippet--Pictorial works. 3. Casanave, Martha. 4. Photography of dogs. I. Title.
   SF429.W5 C27 2002
                                                    2002004678

Published and distributed by the Center for Photographic Art, Carmel, California

The Center for Photographic Art is a nonprofit organization established in 1988, located in Carmel, California. The organization and its programs are supported by memberships, grants and gifts. The Center defines its identity as a photographic fine art organization with a focus on exhibitions, workshops and publications.

Graphic Design: Bert J. Ihlenfeld
Pacific Grove, California

Cover photograph: Martha Casanave
Back cover photograph: Marie Boucher

Printed and bound in China by C&C Offset Printing Co., Ltd